Vanessa Feltz

The Untold Story of a British Television and Radio Personality

Frederick Snow

TABLE OF CONTENTS

INTRODUCTION 6

CHAPTER ONE 13

Early Life and Beginnings 13

Family Background and Heritage 13

Growing Up in Jewish London 15

Early Education and Aspirations 16

The Scholar in Vanessa: Studying English at Cambridge 17

Academic Influences and Early Writing 19

CHAPTER TWO 22

Breaking into Journalism 22

Writing for the Daily Mirror and The Jewish Chronicle 23

Establishing Herself as a Fearless Columnist 25

The Leap from Print Media to TV 26

Behind the Scenes of Early TV Work 28

CHAPTER THREE 31

Television Stardom 31

The Media Storm: Fake Guests Scandal 33

Moving to the BBC and Vanessa 34

Reclaiming Public Trust 35

Hosting The Big Breakfast and Other TV Appearances 36

Other TV and Film Appearances 37

CHAPTER FOUR 39

Radio Royalty 39

Capturing the Audience's Heart: Morning Show Success 40

The National Platform: Radio 2 41

2020s: Evolving Career and New Ventures 45

CHAPTER FIVE 47

Personal Life 47

The Weight Loss Journey: Personal Struggles and Triumphs 50

Family and Home Life 53

CONCLUSION 55

INTRODUCTION

Vanessa Feltz is one of Britain's most enduring and recognizable television and radio personalities, known for her vibrant, often controversial, and ever-candid style. Born on February 21, 1962, in London, Vanessa grew up in a Jewish family in North London, where her personality and flair for communication were evident from an early age. She would go on to attend Haberdashers' Aske's School for Girls before securing a place at the prestigious University of Cambridge, where she studied English Literature. It was here that Vanessa's intellectual curiosity, sharp wit, and gift for articulating ideas were honed, setting the foundation for a career that would span over three decades.

Vanessa's early career began in print journalism, where she contributed columns for several leading publications including The Daily Mirror and The Jewish Chronicle. Her forthright opinions, combined with an engaging writing style, quickly made her a household name in the world of British journalism. However, it wasn't long before her talents for broadcasting saw her shift to television. Vanessa made her first major breakthrough in the early 1990s when she became the host of The Vanessa Show, a daytime talk show that made her a familiar face to millions of viewers. The show was a ratings hit, and Vanessa's unflinching ability to handle difficult topics and her empathetic interviewing style won her legions of fans.

However, her meteoric rise was not without controversy. In 1999, The Vanessa Show became embroiled in a scandal after it was revealed that some of the guests were actors posing as real people. The revelation led to a media storm, and Vanessa was left to face a major career setback. Despite this scandal, Vanessa remained a strong and resilient figure, refusing to be defined by the controversy. She continued to work in television, reinventing herself and her career. She took on new challenges, hosting The Big Breakfast and making regular appearances on This Morning, further establishing herself as a versatile and talented broadcaster.

While Vanessa had already made a name for herself on television, her move to radio in the early 2000s marked a new chapter in her career. Joining BBC Radio London, Vanessa became the voice of the capital's morning radio show, captivating audiences with her no-nonsense approach, humor, and ability to connect with listeners on a deeply personal level. Over the years, she built up a loyal following, and her morning show became one of the station's most popular programs.

Vanessa's success in radio didn't stop at the local level. She went on to host shows on BBC Radio 2, one of the most prestigious platforms in British radio, where her late-night slots offered a mix of music, discussion, and listener interaction. Her candid conversations on topics ranging from relationships to personal challenges resonated with a broad audience, cementing her status as one of the UK's most trusted radio voices.

Beyond her professional achievements, Vanessa Feltz is also known for her larger-than-life personality and her openness about her personal struggles. She has often spoken about her battles with weight, relationships, and the pressures of maintaining a career in the public eye. In particular, her struggles with weight loss have been a frequent topic of discussion, both on her shows and in the media. Vanessa's honesty about her insecurities and her public efforts to shed weight – which included gastric bypass surgery – struck a chord with many people who appreciated her willingness to discuss such personal issues so openly.

In terms of her personal life, Vanessa was married to Michael Kurer, a doctor, in 1983, with whom she had two daughters. However, the couple divorced in 2000, a painful period that Vanessa has spoken about candidly. She found love again with Ben Ofoedu, a musician from the 1990s dance band Phats & Small, and the couple has been together for many years. Their relationship has often been in the spotlight, and Vanessa has shared the ups and downs of their life together, from celebrating milestones to addressing rumors of infidelity.

Despite her occasional stumbles, Vanessa has always displayed an unwavering resilience and determination to keep moving forward. Whether bouncing back from career scandals or navigating personal crises, Vanessa has remained a constant and beloved figure in British entertainment. Her ability to connect with her audience – through both her vulnerability and her strength – has kept her in the public eye long after many of her peers have faded into obscurity.

In addition to her work in broadcasting, Vanessa has also dabbled in reality television. She appeared on Celebrity Big Brother in 2001, where her infamous tantrum involving writing on the walls with chalk is still remembered as one of the most iconic moments in the show's history. Vanessa has also participated in other reality TV ventures such as Strictly Come Dancing, where she showed off her dancing skills to a wide audience, once again displaying her versatility and willingness to step out of her comfort zone.

Throughout her long career, Vanessa has received numerous awards and accolades. She was honored with the Speech Broadcaster of the Year award in 2012 at the Sony Radio Academy Awards, a testament to her skill as a radio presenter and her ability to engage listeners on both lighthearted and serious topics. Her work in television has also been recognized, and she continues to be a regular presence on UK screens, whether as a presenter, commentator, or guest panelist on various programs.

Beyond her professional life, Vanessa has been a vocal advocate for several causes close to her heart. She is a strong supporter of mental health awareness and has often used her platform to speak about the importance of addressing mental health issues openly and without stigma. Vanessa has also been involved in charitable efforts aimed at tackling homelessness, poverty, and domestic abuse, using her public profile to raise awareness and funds for those in need.

Vanessa's life is a story of resilience, adaptability, and the power of authenticity. She has faced significant challenges – from career controversies to personal heartbreak – but has always emerged stronger and more determined. Her ability to reinvent herself, coupled with her unique blend of intelligence, humor, and warmth, has made her a beloved figure across multiple generations of audiences. Today, Vanessa Feltz stands as a testament to what it means to be a true media personality – someone who can entertain, inform, and connect with people on a deeply personal level.

This book will explore Vanessa's life and career in detail, charting her rise from a bright and ambitious young journalist to one of the most enduring figures in British media. Through interviews with those who know her best, alongside Vanessa's own reflections, the book will delve into the highs and lows of her professional and personal life. It will paint a portrait of a woman who, despite the odds, has remained at the top of her game, evolving with the times and continuing to captivate audiences with her unmistakable voice and presence.

Vanessa Feltz's story is one of triumphs, challenges, and the relentless pursuit of success. Her journey – from the scandal surrounding her early talk show to her reinvention as a beloved radio host and reality TV star – offers valuable lessons about the importance of perseverance, authenticity, and the courage to keep going in the face of adversity. Through it all, Vanessa has never lost her sense of humor or her ability to laugh at herself, making her one of the most relatable and admired figures in British media today.

This is her untold story.

CHAPTER ONE

Early Life and Beginnings

Vanessa Feltz's childhood, upbringing, and academic path have all been highly influenced by her family's cultural history, as well as her experiences growing up in a Jewish, middle-class household in North London. Vanessa was born on February 21, 1962, in Islington, London, and grew up in Pine Grove, Totteridge, an affluent neighbourhood she affectionately refers to as "the Beverly Hills of North London." This description captures not only her wealthy upbringing, but also her sharp wit and self-awareness, qualities that would eventually define her broadcasting career.

Family Background and Heritage

Vanessa is from a Jewish family, and her heritage has always been a significant part of her identity. Her father, Norman Feltz, owned a successful lingerie business that helped the family make a decent living. Vanessa's drive for achievement was most likely inspired by her father's entrepreneurial attitude and work ethic. While Norman's business was not a flashy one, it offered financial stability for the family, allowing them to live in Totteridge, a neighborhood known for its verdant avenues and big homes.

Vanessa's mother, Valerie Feltz, had an important role in her upbringing, teaching in her the value of education, tradition, and community. Vanessa's mother was more concerned with the domestic aspects of life, such as creating a safe and caring environment, but she equally valued academic performance, which would have a significant impact on her future. Valerie was known for her kindness and support, which Vanessa accentuated later in life, especially in relation to her own role as a mother.

Vanessa's sister, Julia, is three years younger than her. Growing up, the two siblings had a deep friendship and explored the world extensively. Vanessa has regularly stressed her bond with Julia, noting her sister as someone who helps her stay grounded amongst her growing media celebrity. Despite their affluence, the Feltz family upheld many traditional traditions, with their Jewish heritage playing a significant role in their everyday lives. Vanessa had a strong sense of cultural connection and community belonging when she followed Jewish traditions and celebrations on a regular basis.

Growing Up in Jewish London

Vanessa's upbringing in North London during the 1960s and 1970s was profoundly affected by her Jewish heritage and the area's vibrant Jewish culture. Vanessa was nurtured in an environment where Jewish traditions and practices were seamlessly integrated into everyday life. North London, particularly Totteridge and the surrounding areas, has long had a large Jewish community.

She described her childhood as "growing up in Fiddler on the Roof," referring to the popular musical about Jewish families in early twentieth-century Russia. While the analogy is amusing and overused, it highlights Vanessa's strong connection to Jewish culture and how it has affected her viewpoint. Her family was not extremely religious, but they practiced many Jewish rites and traditions. Vanessa experienced a profound sense of connection and belonging as a result of the Feltz family's monthly Shabbat dinners, holiday celebrations, and community gatherings.

Vanessa's Jewish upbringing prepared her for the challenges of being a minority in a predominantly non-Jewish town. Anti-Semitism was not a huge issue in her personal life, but she was well aware of it, and her upbringing in a Jewish household most likely influenced her later work as a journalist and broadcaster, in which she continually spoke out against prejudice and discrimination in all forms.

Early Education and Aspirations

Vanessa's early education was equally enriching as her childhood. She attended Haberdashers' Aske's School for Girls, a prestigious private school in Elstree, Hertfordshire, known for its academic rigour and high standards. Vanessa's school provided a solid foundation for both academics and extracurricular activities, nurturing her talents and honing her intellectual curiosity.

Vanessa took an early interest in literature and writing. Her teachers at Haberdashers' rapidly recognized her intellectual abilities and love of language, helping her to excel in English and other humanities studies. Vanessa has frequently remarked how much she enjoyed school, when she discovered a love of reading and writing that she has kept with her throughout her life. During her school years, she developed an interest in public speaking and debating, which she would later use in her broadcasting career.

Vanessa started fantasizing about a job in journalism or radio, which was rare for a girl in her community. Nonetheless, her family supported her ambitions, particularly her father, who encouraged her to pursue her academic and professional aspirations with the same zeal with which he had created his own successful business. Vanessa's parents valued education and achievement, and they taught her that she could accomplish everything she set her mind to.

The Scholar in Vanessa: Studying English at Cambridge

Vanessa's academic journey began at Haberdashers' Aske's School for Girls and eventually took her to Trinity College, Cambridge, one of the world's most prestigious institutions. This was a remarkable achievement because admission to Cambridge was (and still is) extraordinarily difficult, especially for a middle-class female.

Vanessa studied English at Cambridge, where she was able to immerse herself in the realm of literature, something she had always enjoyed. Her time at Cambridge was transformative, both academically and personally. Vanessa excelled in her college's challenging academic environment. She was known for her sharp intellect and quick wit, which earned her the respect of her peers and professors.

Vanessa was influenced by some of the most famous literary experts of her day while studying at Cambridge, and this period of her life significantly broadened her understanding of literature and language. The university's stimulating intellectual environment, combined with her natural curiosity and enthusiasm for learning, helped her develop a nuanced and sophisticated approach to writing and communication.

Vanessa's time at Cambridge also allowed her to participate in extracurricular activities that helped shape her eventual career path. She participated in debates and discussions, refining her public speaking skills and gaining the confidence that would later push her to such prominence on television and radio. Vanessa was also able to exhibit her artistic side at Cambridge, which encouraged her to pursue a career in media, writing, and journalism.

Vanessa remained interested in writing throughout her undergraduate years. She wrote for student publications and took part in discussions about literature, culture, and society, which helped her intellectual and communicative development. Her academic work was of such high quality that she received a first-class honors degree in English, a remarkable achievement that set her apart from her peers and opened the door to a variety of professional opportunities.

Academic Influences and Early Writing

Vanessa's academic experience at Cambridge shaped her future career as a journalist and broadcaster. She studied with some of the most influential literary educators of her time, and their courses inspired her to think critically about literature and society. This academic rigor, along with her natural desire to speak, laid the groundwork for her future success in the media industry.

Her early work reflected her enthusiasm for language and storytelling. Vanessa's work was intellectual, inventive, and frequently amusing, even while she was a student. Her ability to combine intellectual depth and an engaging, conversational tone would later distinguish her as a presenter and columnist.

Vanessa's early writing shows an interest in societal issues. She was drawn to topics of the human condition, cultural identity, and the challenges of modern life. These subjects would soon dominate her career as a journalist and radio personality, where she addressed controversial and thought-provoking matters with candor and sensitivity.

Vanessa was never pleased with her academic performance. She had a great desire to reach a bigger audience and saw journalism and radio as viable platforms for spreading her ideas and engaging the public. Her experience at Cambridge had amply prepared her for this endeavor, giving her the intellectual ability and confidence needed to thrive in the extremely competitive field of journalism.

To recapitulate, Vanessa Feltz's early life and academic career were marked by a strong sense of cultural identity, intellectual curiosity, and a desire to succeed. Her Jewish upbringing in North London, her education at Haberdashers' Aske's School for Girls, and her years studying English at Cambridge all shaped who she was. These formative events laid the framework for Vanessa's incredible broadcasting career, during which her acute intelligence, wit, and daring propelled her to become one of the most recognized and respected voices in British media.

CHAPTER TWO

Breaking into Journalism

Vanessa Feltz's enthusiasm for language and storytelling inspired her to seek a career in journalism. After graduating from Cambridge University, where she studied English Literature, she wanted to use her academic knowledge in real-world journalism. Her first foray into print journalism began when she was offered a position at The Jewish Chronicle, the UK's oldest and most well-known Jewish daily.

Vanessa Feltz, a young journalist, has already established provocative viewpoints and a consistent style. She was The Jewish Chronicle's first female columnist, which was an impressive feat in the 1980s, when journalism was still mostly male-dominated. Her essays in The Jewish Chronicle were witty, intelligent, and frequently challenging, covering topics ranging from social difficulties to cultural criticism. She did not sidestep controversy, openly questioning Jewish identity, gender norms, and the changing dynamics of the community.

Writing for the Daily Mirror and The Jewish Chronicle

Vanessa Feltz started her journalism career at The Jewish Chronicle, but her goals didn't stop there. She quickly attracted to larger, more visible platforms. Her unusual voice piqued the interest of editors at The Daily Mirror, one of the UK's most well-known national newspapers. The Daily Mirror was known for its left-leaning editorials and populist tone, which Feltz's daring, occasionally aggressive writing enhanced.

Feltz quickly made a name for herself at The Daily Mirror by tackling topics that others might neglect, and doing it with humor and insight that appealed to a huge audience. Her articles offered a realistic perspective on daily life, frequently criticizing the shortcomings of modern civilization while also addressing big social and political issues. Whether she was discussing celebrity culture, family life, or politics, her writing was engaging, sharp, and impossible to ignore.

During this time, Feltz's reputation as a controversial columnist grew. Her writing did not shy away from difficult or sensitive topics, and she built a loyal readership who appreciated her no-holds-barred attitude. Feltz excelled at incorporating humor into her criticism, which enabled her to connect with readers on a deeper level.

During this period, she also released her first novel, "What Are These Strawberries Doing to My Nipples?" I Need Them for the Fruit Salad was a humorous and provocative title that exemplified Feltz's willingness to push the boundaries and welcome controversy. The book, like her articles, was brimming with wit and humor, offering a fun yet biting commentary on all aspects of life, relationships, and contemporary culture. It cemented her public image as a writer who isn't afraid to express herself and has a unique ability to blend the personal and political in ways that appeal with her readers.

Feltz's move from The Jewish Chronicle to The Daily Mirror boosted her visibility and capacity to cover a broader variety of issues. While her work at The Jewish Chronicle focused on the Jewish community and cultural issues, The Daily Mirror gave her the opportunity to reach a larger audience and cover a wider range of topics. This dual experience, writing for both a small, community-focused magazine and a large, national daily, gave Feltz a distinct perspective that she would employ later in her television career.

Establishing Herself as a Fearless Columnist

Feltz's time at The Daily Mirror saw her develop from a competent writer to a bold columnist whose opinions sparked debate and, on occasion, scandal. Her ability to handle sensitive topics, often with stinging humor, distinguished her from the crowd of columnists. She covered everything from celebrity scandals to political gaffes, giving readers a keen, no-nonsense perspective. Her writing was usually infused with personal experiences, giving it a compassionate, conversational tone that helped her gain popularity among readers.

At the Daily Mirror, Feltz demonstrated her versatility. She could effortlessly transition from serious social critique to light-hearted celebrity gossip, indicating that she was just as comfortable arguing the latest political topic as she was criticizing the latest fashion or entertainment fads. Her severe, honest tone positioned her as a must-read columnist, and her readership grew rapidly.

Feltz was not scared of controversy, and her time at The Daily Mirror was marked by a number of high-profile disputes with public people who disagreed with her views. Instead of avoiding criticism, Feltz embraced it and used it to fuel her next initiative. Her outspokenness gained her a reputation as a journalist who could be both amusing and thought-provoking, something many of her colleagues struggled with.

Her columns proved her understanding of the present zeitgeist. Feltz has an exceptional capacity to understand people's opinions, addressing topics that were both timely and frequently hot. Her work echoed her readers' concerns and interests, catapulting her from critic to cultural barometer. She was not afraid to express opinions that others might have found offensive, and her willingness to break from the standard only added to her appeal.

The Leap from Print Media to TV

Feltz had established herself as a writer and columnist, but she refused to stay in print. Her engaging personality and sharp wit made her a perfect choice for television, and she switched from print to broadcasting in the early 1990s.

Her television career began with appearances on talk shows and panel debates, where her quick wit and outspoken personality made her a popular guest. Producers saw Feltz's potential as a television personality who could attract audiences and spark passionate debate. It wasn't long until she was offered her own television show, The Vanessa Show, which aired on ITV.

The Vanessa Show was a midday chat show that included celebrity interviews, discussions on current affairs, and audience involvement. Feltz's journalism background paid dividends in this new format, allowing her to ask probing questions and provide in-depth analysis while keeping the show's tone light and engaging.

However, the shift from paper to television was not seamless. Feltz quickly learned that television was a different beast from print journalism, with its own set of demands and pressures. The fast-paced nature of live television required her to think quickly and react to unexpected situations. Unlike print, where she could carefully organize her words, television required spontaneity and the ability to communicate with an audience in real time.

Despite these hurdles, Feltz thrived in her new role as a television personality. Her sharp wit and honest demeanor worked well on television, and she quickly developed a devoted following. The Vanessa Show format allowed her to showcase her journalistic ability on television, asking difficult questions and discussing delicate topics in terms that daytime viewers could comprehend.

Feltz's shift to television allowed her to reach a much broader audience than she did as a columnist. While her work at The Daily Mirror and The Jewish Chronicle earned her a dedicated readership, television introduced her to millions of households in the United Kingdom. Her candid, often humorous, demeanor charmed a large audience, and she swiftly climbed to popularity on daytime television.

Behind the Scenes of Early TV Work

Behind the scenes, Feltz's early television work was frenzy of planning, stress, and snap decisions. Hosting a live television show required her to master new skills, such as pacing the interview and dealing with technological issues. Unlike print journalism, where Feltz had unlimited control over her words and the outcome, television was significantly less predictable. Guests may have noticed that unforeseen technology glitches disturbed the concert's flow, and Feltz must learn to deal with such challenges calmly and effectively.

One of the most challenging components of her early television career was combining entertainment with journalistic ethics. As a journalist, Feltz was accustomed to diving into issues and providing well-researched, nuanced viewpoints. However, daytime television requires a softer touch, so Feltz had to adapt her technique to the medium. She needed to keep the show interesting while yet addressing important subjects, which she mastered over time.

Despite these challenges, Feltz's early television work was a success, and she quickly established herself as one of the UK's most well-known television personalities. Her ability to connect with both her guests and viewers, combined with her quick wit and journalistic instincts, propelled her to the forefront of daytime television's most recognizable faces.

Vanessa Feltz's transition from print to television marked a watershed moment in her career, driving her to become a household name in Britain. Her early television work drew heavily on her journalism background, allowing her to bring a unique blend of intelligence, wit, and aggressiveness to the screen. As her television career evolved, Feltz continued to push the boundaries and challenge expectations, cementing her image as one of the most dynamic figures in British media.

CHAPTER THREE

Television Stardom

Vanessa Feltz rose to prominence during the mid-1990s television series The Vanessa Show. The show, which focused on typical issues faced by everyday people, capitalized on the British public's interest in reality television and human drama. It included visitors who shared their own tales, which were mostly about family issues, romantic disputes, and other sensitive matters.

The format of the show was based on the enormously successful American talk show circuit, which featured superstars such as Oprah Winfrey, but with a distinct British twist. Unlike its American counterparts, The Vanessa Show took a more reserved approach, with Feltz serving as a facilitator rather than originator. She displayed genuine empathy, which enabled her to connect with the visitors and make them feel heard and understood.

The presentation style was basic but effective, with the intention of reaching a big audience. Vanessa would start each episode by introducing the guests and then hosting an open discussion in which they could share their personal struggles. She grabbed the audience with her easygoing charm and intellectual curiosity, making her a popular option among daytime television viewers.

Despite its popularity, The Vanessa Show was not without challenges. One of the most significant concerns occurred in 1999, when it was revealed that some of the show's guests were actors dealing with personal issues. This revelation generated a media frenzy, leaving many viewers feeling misled by what they thought was a legitimate debate presentation.

Feltz's reputation suffered as a result of the affair, despite the fact that she was not personally responsible for the phony guests. A different staffer handled the guest booking, and Feltz had no idea the participants were actors. However, as the show's face, she drew the most criticism, with many accusing her of complicity or negligence. This argument led to the cancellation of the show, which was a low point in her career.

At the time, daytime talk shows were often seen as pushing the boundaries of entertainment and ethics. The line between real-life drama and produced entertainment had gotten increasingly blurry, and The Vanessa Show was one of the casualties. Vanessa maintained she had no say in the guest scheduling decisions, but the damage to her reputation had already been done. After the show was canceled, Feltz faced a professional crossroads.

The Media Storm: Fake Guests Scandal

The phony guest incident on The Vanessa Show tarnished Vanessa's reputation while also sparking a broader debate about the ethics of reality TV. In an era when talk shows thrived on sensationalized content, some people felt driven to go overboard. The Vanessa Show became a symbol of this movement, but it was not the only one causing problems.

The controversy erupted after a newspaper investigated and discovered that some of the show's guests were paid to play specific roles on the show, such as fabricating fictitious stories to increase drama and attract viewers. This revelation startled viewers who had been duped into believing it was a genuine, unscripted conversation show.

Feltz was considered as the incident's public face despite having no direct involvement in the fraud. In public, she was found guilty of association. The tabloids seized on the story, casting Feltz as a key participant in the disaster. The extensive media coverage had an emotional impact on her, but it also drove her to rebuild her career and reputation.

Moving to the BBC and Vanessa

Following the cancelation of The Vanessa Show, Feltz's next move was important. She deliberately switched from ITV to the BBC, where she was allocated to the new debate show Vanessa. The move was notable for both the network relocation and the rumored £2.7 million payout. The big contract indicated that, despite the controversy around her, Vanessa Feltz was still a bankable name on British television.

Vanessa followed a similar approach to her previous show, but the BBC's more regulated and serious tone helped her re-establish her image. Despite the challenges, the BBC chose Feltz because they believed she could connect with the audience. The new show also helped her regain public trust by avoiding the sensationalism that had damaged The Vanessa Show.

Vanessa, on the other hand, struggled to sustain the popularity of her ITV show. The issue surrounding her last talk show continued, and viewership fell short of expectations. Despite these challenges, Feltz was determined to resume her broadcasting career.

Reclaiming Public Trust

Vanessa Feltz had great obstacles in rebuilding public trust. Following the crisis, she had to work hard to demonstrate to viewers that she was still a trustworthy and effective broadcaster. One way she accomplished this was to return to her journalism roots and concentrate on vital issues requiring her intellect and emotional intelligence.

In interviews, Feltz admitted to having difficulties and accepted responsibility for her public image, despite the fact that she was not directly responsible for The Vanessa Show's bogus guests. Her candor regarding the subject, as well as her willingness to accept her mistakes in public, helped her gain the support of some audiences who admired her honesty.

Feltz also used her platform to talk about personal issues including her weight struggles and life as a mother and wife.

Her openness about her personal life made her more approachable, and she eventually won back the public's trust. Vanessa's perseverance, both professionally and personally, became a distinguishing feature of her public image.

Hosting The Big Breakfast and Other TV Appearances

Vanessa Feltz took on a new challenge in 1997, when she joined Channel 4's popular morning show The Big Breakfast. She succeeded Paula Yates, who had previously hosted the show's popular segment when she interviewed celebrities while lying in bed. Vanessa brought her own distinct flavor to the role, delivering interviews with wit, compassion, and honesty that captivated the show's audience.

However, this period of her career was not without controversy. Vanessa alleges that Rolf Harris, a disgraced TV personality, sexually harassed her while she was interviewing him for The Big Breakfast. The remark was made far later in her career, as part of a larger national conversation about abuse in the entertainment industry. Vanessa's decision to speak out about her experience exposed the complexities of her public image, which depicted her as both powerful and empathetic.

Vanessa rose to prominence after appearing on a number of comic TV shows, including The Big Breakfast. For example, in 1997, she was misled by the satirical TV show Brass Eye, which criticized journalists and politicians. While this may have harmed her reputation, Vanessa handled it gently, demonstrating her ability to laugh at herself and not take things too seriously.

Vanessa, in addition to her TV profession, has been a magistrate since the age of 28. Her work as a magistrate demonstrated her commitment to public service and justice, but as her television profile grew, she found it more difficult to remain impartial. Defendants recognized her from television appearances, and it was clear that her function as a public personality conflicted with her legal responsibilities. She was asked to step down, which marked the end of an important chapter in her life.

Other TV and Film Appearances

Vanessa had numerous appearances on British television during the 2000s, both as a presenter and as a cast member in various shows. In 2001, she made a cameo appearance in the comedy film Once Upon a Time in the Midlands, demonstrating her ability to spoof herself.

She has also been in game shows, notably an episode of Russian Roulette hosted by comedian Rhona Cameron. Vanessa's ability to shift from serious news to lighter topics demonstrated her versatility as a media personality.

Vanessa Feltz has been persistent throughout her career. Her capacity to reinvent herself following a calamity and restart her career exemplifies her tenacity and adaptability as a media figure. Vanessa's climb from tabloid outrage to respected broadcaster proves that, while celebrity is fleeting, hard effort and genuineness can help rehabilitate a career and regain public trust.

CHAPTER FOUR

Radio Royalty

Feltz began his broadcasting career with BBC Broadcast London. Vanessa took over the morning show in 2001, bringing her unique blend of wit, sharp intellect, and emotional connection to her audience. Her presence on the airwaves quickly became more than just another announcer shouting into a microphone. Listeners developed a personal connection with Vanessa. Her friendly voice, combined with candid discussions about everything from current events to personal experiences, helped her establish herself as a new type of radio personality: approachable but authoritative.

Her show became an essential component of Londoners' morning routines. Feltz's show provided a unique forum for debate and discussion on a variety of themes, including politics and personal experiences. Vanessa's ability to balance amusing moments with serious topics was critical to her success, whether she was dealing with political concerns, researching everyday human stories, or expressing her own struggles.

She was never hesitant to talk about her family life, weight reduction struggles, and personal relationships. Her candor drew a devoted following, who valued her relatability and honesty. Her openness about her Jewish origin lent a unique perspective to discussions about identity, faith, and culture, allowing listeners to connect with issues that are typically disregarded by mainstream media.

Capturing the Audience's Heart: Morning Show Success

Vanessa's success on BBC Radio London stemmed in large part from her ability to make her listeners feel heard. She encouraged live calls and established an environment in which listeners could express themselves, tell their stories, and contribute to the discussion. Her approach went beyond just providing data and included engaging, conversing, and connecting on a personal level. This deep bond drew a devoted following.

Her morning show, which ran from 9 a.m. until 12 p.m., became a cornerstone of BBC Radio London's programming. People tuned in not simply to hear the latest news, but also to feel a part of the larger community that

Vanessa had built on-air. Her success on the show cemented her reputation as a prominent figure in British radio, and by the early 2010s, she was widely considered as one of the most popular local radio broadcasters.

But Vanessa's goals didn't end there. Her morning show's expanding success demonstrated her ability to handle larger audiences, resulting her possibilities on national radio.

The National Platform: Radio 2

Vanessa's radio career skyrocketed in 2011, when she took over the BBC Radio 2 Early Breakfast Show. Feltz, who succeeded Sarah Kennedy, began broadcasting every weekday between 5:00 and 6:30 a.m. Vanessa's climb from local radio to national prominence was remarkable. Vanessa's early breakfast show became important listening for many people in the UK, and she rose to prominence during this tough time.

Both critics and fans loved her singing and style. Gillian Reynolds of The Daily Telegraph accurately described Feltz's voice as "like lemon tea with honey," nailing the calming yet brisk tone she brought to the early morning. Vanessa's ability to blend lighter humor with more serious subjects was continuous throughout her programming, and even at such an early hour, her show never failed to elicit heated debate.

The early morning visit presented some difficulties, but Vanessa's excitement and comprehension shined through. Her strong work ethic gained her a reputation in the industry, with some calling her "the hardest working woman in broadcasting." Managing the early breakfast broadcast, in addition to her other responsibilities at BBC Radio London, required tremendous stamina and dedication.

Vanessa's show was extended by one hour in 2021, beginning at 4:00 a.m. This presented her with a unique opportunity to interact with her audience, and she rose to the situation. During her stay, she also covered the popular Jeremy Vine Show while Vine was away, solidifying her position as one of Radio 2's most versatile presenters. Her ease with challenging news and current affairs themes endeared her to a large audience.

Vanessa, on the other hand, decided to leave Radio 2's early breakfast show after almost a decade in charge. In July 2022, she announced her departure from Radio 2, leaving a legacy of high-quality programming and a devoted fan following. She remained at Radio 2 for a bit longer, covering for Jeremy Vine until August 2022, when she departed the station.

Vanessa's open attitude toward broadcasting helped her advance in her radio profession. Unlike many presenters who keep a formal distance from their audience, Vanessa was always open and vulnerable, giving personal tales and insights that drew her in. Whether she was discussing her weight loss journey, her experiences as a mother and grandmother, or more personal themes like relationships and self-esteem, Feltz never hesitated to be herself on television.

This honesty became her signature. They felt as if they knew her personally, rather than just hearing her voice on the radio. This genuine connection is what keeps viewers engaged day after day. Vanessa's performances created an environment in which people felt free to express their views, knowing they would be acknowledged and accepted.

Vanessa Feltz is most known for her radio and television work, but she has also had a significant presence on reality television, where she frequently portrays a different version of herself.

Vanessa appeared in the first season of Celebrity Big Brother in 2001, a reality TV show that partnered celebrities to live in a house under constant supervision. Vanessa's experience in the Big Brother house was memorable, to say the least. One of the most memorable moments was when she had a breakdown and started writing on a table with lipstick, which will go down in reality TV history.

Despite being constantly observed, Vanessa's performance on the show demonstrated her sensitivity and honesty. Her willingness to express her true emotions, even in the high-pressure setting of reality TV, helped her become a beloved character among viewers.

Vanessa returns to the Big Brother house for the 2010 season finale of Channel 4's Ultimate Big Brother. She returned to the house on September 3, 2010, but was ousted just five days later, on September 8, two days before the final.

Vanessa appeared on the popular reality TV show Strictly Come Dancing in 2013. Vanessa, accompanied by professional dancer James Jordan, brought her usual enthusiasm and enjoyment to the dance floor. Vanessa's debut performance on the show was both amusing and interesting, despite the fact that her dancing abilities were not as widely known as her broadcasting abilities. She was eliminated in the third week, but her appearance on Strictly has increased her reputation.

Vanessa's career progressed gradually throughout the years. In 2011, she was promoted to a more senior position, with responsibility for both radio and television. On March 7, 2011, Channel 5 shifted The Vanessa Show to the afternoon, allowing her to continue making live television appearances despite her morning radio schedule. Although the show's ratings rose, a second season was planned but never materialized.

Vanessa remained a major personality in the British media well into the 2010s. In 2019, she was named one of the top ten highest-paid BBC presenters, together with Claudia Winkleman and Zoe Ball, earning an estimated £355,000.

2020s: Evolving Career and New Ventures

Vanessa continued to dominate the airwaves into the 2020s, but not without controversy. In 2024, she stirred outrage with statements about celiac disease on This Morning, resulting in over 2,000 complaints to Ofcom. Vanessa apologized for her statements, demonstrating her willingness to take responsibility and move forward.

Vanessa began hosting the daily drivetime show on Talkradio and TalkTV after leaving BBC Radio 2 in 2022, allowing her to continue showcasing her broadcasting abilities. Then, in May 2024, she agreed to anchor a Saturday afternoon show on LBC, cementing her reputation as one of the most well-known figures in British radio.

Vanessa has appeared as a wrestling pundit on Late Night Lycett and wrestled in a Kamikaze Pro event, demonstrating her enthusiasm to face new challenges.

CHAPTER FIVE

Personal Life

Vanessa Feltz's personal life has been as dramatic and public as her career, encompassing love and loss, triumphs and tragedies. Her public partnerships represent a strong and determined woman who has openly acknowledged concerns of love, commitment, and separation.

In 1983, Feltz married surgeon Michael Kurer. Their marriage seemed stable for many years, and they produced two children, Allegra and Saskia. Feltz frequently spoke fondly about her family life, painting an image of a contented and prosperous household. However, the couple divorced in 2000, 17 years after they married. The separation was quick and public, with Feltz admitting Kurer abandoned her with little notice. Vanessa dealt with the emotional impact of her failed marriage while caring for her two young daughters, Allegra and Saskia.

The dissolution of her marriage had a profound emotional impact on her. Vanessa openly confessed that her relationship ended unexpectedly, exacerbating her sense of betrayal. Divorce is a very personal and emotional event for many women, particularly those in the public glare, and Vanessa's was no different. Rather than fleeing the spotlight, she stayed in her position, gaining strength from her own experiences. She found peace in her profession and focused on her daughters, creating strong ties with Allegra and Saskia.

Despite the heartbreak, Vanessa's tenacity in the face of adversity remained a defining feature of her public image. She was frank about her emotions, sharing her difficulties in interviews and on the radio, which touched many people. This was a watershed moment in her life, and she started to reconstruct herself emotionally.

In December 2006, Feltz got engaged to Ben Ofoedu, the main singer of Phats & Small. The couple immediately rose to public fame, with their relationship garnering widespread coverage in tabloids and other media outlets. Originally, they planned to marry the next year, but the wedding was postponed and never happened. Despite this, Vanessa and Ben remained engaged for several years and attended a variety of events together.

Ben Ofoedu, known for his positive nature and musical career, appeared to rekindle Vanessa's enthusiasm and friendship. Vanessa complimented Ben for his support and their strong emotional bond, demonstrating that the couple was truly in love. For many years, their relationship appeared to be one of stability and mutual admiration, making their abrupt split in February 2023 all the more surprising to the public.

Vanessa revealed that she and Ben will split in early 2023. The split occurred after many years of being together, and it was widely reported in the media, with speculation about the reasons for the breakup. Vanessa kept an honest tone and candidly discussed their breakup, showing that she was both devastated and ready to move on. Vanessa's breakup signified the end of an important chapter in her life, but as with all other situations, she addressed it with her usual zeal.

Vanessa Feltz's willingness to be transparent about her personal life is evident in her relationships and marriage. She has shared her highs and lows with the world, providing a unique viewpoint on the complexity of love, dedication, and heartbreak. Her desire to reveal personal information in a genuine and honest manner has garnered her a significant fan base, transforming her into not only a television and radio personality, but also a relatable figure who connects with her audience on a deep level.

The Weight Loss Journey: Personal Struggles and Triumphs

Vanessa Feltz has spoken openly about her weight issues for many years, including her challenges with body image, health, and self-esteem. Her quest for a better life has been a prominent element throughout her journey, which she frequently discusses in interviews and on the radio. Vanessa's weight loss was motivated not only by her physical looks, but also by her mental health, confidence, and sense of self-worth.

Vanessa Feltz has struggled with weight throughout her career. She has openly discussed how her changing weight has affected her personally and professionally. As a well-known media figure, she was frequently scrutinized for her appearance, and she felt compelled to meet strict beauty standards. Vanessa expressed concern and frustration over the constant focus on her weight.

Vanessa's weight problems reached a critical stage when she decided to take charge of her health. In the mid-2010s, she began a substantial weight-loss quest, shedding approximately three stone. The metamorphosis caused physical and mental changes. Vanessa described the therapy as liberating, not only because of the obvious changes in her appearance, but also because she felt more energized and confident. She described how decreasing weight transformed her perspective, gave her more control over her life, and helped her overcome unpleasant emotions she had been dealing with for years.

Vanessa's gastric band surgery was a key step toward meeting her weight loss objectives and leading a healthy lifestyle. Vanessa considered the operation to be a difficult decision due to its importance. She honestly articulated the emotional consequences of her decision, recognizing that it was not a short fix, but rather a tool to assist her reach a long-term objective. Vanessa's operation, combined with proper diet and an active lifestyle, resulted in significant weight loss, allowing her to lose several stones and restore confidence.

Vanessa's trip was not without hurdles. She discussed the difficulties of maintaining her weight loss and the psychological challenges that accompanied it. Vanessa, like many others who have lost a considerable amount of weight, has had to constantly work on her relationship with food and body image. The obligations of being in the spotlight made her journey even more difficult, as she was often ridiculed for her appearance, both before and after she lost weight.

Despite her obstacles, Vanessa has become a role model for many people who struggle with their weight and body image. She utilized her platform to convey the realities of weight loss—both the successes and the setbacks—and how it is a journey rather than a goal. Many of her supporters enjoyed her openness about the process, including the emotional elements of weight loss.

Vanessa's weight loss journey displays her determination and perseverance. It encapsulates her entire approach to life, in which she confronts obstacles full on and is not hesitant to share her struggles publicly. Her ability to turn personal tragedies into meaningful and inspiring stories has propelled her to prominence in British media, where she is recognized not just for her professional accomplishments but also for her ability to overcome personal obstacles.

Family and Home Life

Vanessa Feltz's professional and personal lives have garnered a lot of attention, but her role as a mother and grandmother is essential to her identity. She has two daughters from her marriage to Michael Kurer: Allegra and Saskia. Her eldest daughter, Allegra Benitah, started her career as a tax lawyer, following in her father's footsteps. Allegra eventually became a TV baker and chef, forging her own identity in the media industry. Vanessa expressed delight in her children's accomplishments and abilities to establish their own paths.

Vanessa is not only a mother, but also a dedicated grandma to her four grandchildren, whom she adores. She is constantly talking about how much she enjoys spending time with her grandchildren and how becoming a grandmother has given her life new meaning. Despite her hectic schedule, Vanessa values family, emphasizing the value of her personal relationships with her children and grandchildren.

Vanessa Feltz lives in a historically significant property in St. John's Wood, London. The property was previously owned by art dealer Charles Saatchi and appeared in Sir John Betjeman's 1973 documentary Metro-Land. Vanessa's diverse interests and passion for history and culture are reflected in her home, which serves as a retreat from the media glare. Vanessa regards her home as more than simply a physical structure; it represents security and continuity, particularly in light of recent personal changes.

Vanessa Feltz's family life, albeit somewhat private, is an important aspect of her personality. Despite the difficulties she has encountered in relationships, her closeness to her children and grandchildren provides her a feeling of fulfillment and purpose. Vanessa has maintained a close relationship with her family throughout the ups and downs, and it remains one of her primary sources of strength and happiness.

CONCLUSION

Vanessa Feltz's journey is emblematic of perseverance, charisma, and a love for communication that transcends mere entertainment. Her life in the public eye has not just been about presenting or entertaining, but about authenticity—an unwavering desire to share both the highs and lows with her audience. From the early days of her journalism career to her omnipresence on television and radio, Vanessa has embodied resilience and an indomitable spirit, even when faced with personal and professional challenges that would have daunted many.

Feltz's story, which began in the bustling streets of North London, provides a vivid reminder of the transformative power of determination. Raised in a Jewish household, her upbringing instilled in her the values of hard work, self-expression, and community, which would become the bedrock of her career in media. But more than that, her sharp wit and intellectual prowess, honed during her time at Cambridge, set her apart early on as a formidable force in journalism. Her decision to move from the written word to television was not just a career pivot, but a declaration of her intent to connect more deeply with the public.

Vanessa's move into television was, for many, the defining moment of her career. The Vanessa Show was groundbreaking at the time, a space where real issues were tackled with sensitivity and sincerity. It allowed ordinary people to tell their stories and be heard—something Vanessa knew was integral to human connection. Unfortunately, the scandal that rocked the show in the late 1990s, where it was revealed that some of the guests were actors, could have easily spelled the end of her career. But instead, it became a turning point. Vanessa's ability to weather the storm, admit fault where necessary, and rebuild her career with integrity speaks volumes about her character.

The scandal was a learning experience, not just for Feltz but for the entire industry. It raised questions about the authenticity of reality television, the ethics of production, and the delicate balance between entertainment and truth. In navigating this treacherous terrain, Vanessa showed remarkable strength. She made it clear that while mistakes happen, they do not define a person. This capacity to grow, evolve, and learn has been one of the cornerstones of her longevity in an industry that is notoriously fickle.

Her transition to radio, particularly her long-standing tenure at BBC Radio London, was a masterstroke. In the often impersonal world of modern broadcasting, Vanessa brought something many presenters struggle to achieve—intimacy. Whether she was discussing the news of the day or diving deep into personal anecdotes about her own life, Vanessa had an innate ability to make listeners feel as though they were chatting with a trusted friend. Her show was a comforting presence for many, providing a blend of warmth, humor, and incisive commentary on current events and social issues.

Vanessa's radio work also allowed her to showcase her versatility as a broadcaster. While her television persona was often tied to the controversies and sensationalism of talk shows, radio gave her the space to be more reflective, engaging in thoughtful dialogue with listeners on topics ranging from politics to pop culture to mental health. This was where her true gift for communication shone through—not as a purveyor of drama, but as a facilitator of meaningful conversation. Her audience was not passive; they were collaborators in the ongoing dialogue that her show fostered.

Moreover, her stint on BBC Radio 2's early morning show brought her voice to a wider audience, further cementing her place in British broadcasting. It is not easy to keep listeners engaged during the early hours, but Vanessa did so with grace, wit, and an unwavering sense of responsibility toward her audience. She made waking up at ungodly hours something to look forward to for many Britons.

Reality television has become a major part of Vanessa's public life, but it would be too simplistic to say she participated merely for fame. Her appearances on shows like Celebrity Big Brother and Strictly Come Dancing offered an intriguing glimpse into the woman behind the public persona. These programs gave audiences a chance to see Vanessa as a human being, with vulnerabilities, quirks, and a sense of humor that often got lost in the tabloid portrayal of her as a media "diva."

In Celebrity Big Brother, Vanessa's breakdown became one of the most talked-about moments in the show's history. But it wasn't the spectacle that mattered—it was the aftermath.

Once again, Vanessa showed the world that being in the public eye does not mean you're invincible. Her raw emotion was not a sign of weakness, but of her deep-seated passion and humanity. She has always been open about her struggles with mental health, and her willingness to discuss these challenges publicly has undoubtedly helped destigmatize the issue for many of her listeners and viewers.

Her participation in Strictly Come Dancing showcased a different side of Vanessa—one that embraced challenge and fun. While not a natural dancer, she threw herself into the competition with the same zeal that had defined her career in media. It was this willingness to try, to take risks even when the odds were stacked against her, that endeared her to a whole new generation of fans.

In her personal life, Vanessa has faced significant challenges, from the public breakdown of her marriage to the relentless scrutiny that comes with being a tabloid target. Her relationship with surgeon Michael Kurer ended in a very public divorce, a traumatic experience that she handled with remarkable dignity. Rather than retreating from the spotlight, Vanessa chose to confront the pain head-on, sharing her story with her audience and offering solidarity to others going through similar hardships.

Her long-term partnership with singer Ben Ofoedu has also been a subject of public interest. Despite the age difference and the inevitable gossip that surrounds high-profile relationships, Vanessa has always maintained that love is about connection and understanding, not appearances. Their relationship has been a testament to her belief in living authentically and without fear of judgment.

Her candid discussions about weight, self-esteem, and body image have also resonated deeply with her audience, particularly in a media landscape that often places an unhealthy emphasis on physical appearance. Vanessa's openness about her struggles with weight loss, combined with her refusal to conform to societal standards of beauty, has made her a role model for many. She represents the idea that self-worth is not tied to size, and that true confidence comes from embracing who you are.

Vanessa Feltz's impact on British media cannot be overstated. She has been a trailblazer in many respects—a Jewish woman who carved out a space for herself in the often male-dominated world of broadcasting, a public figure who has never shied away from speaking her truth, and a presenter who has always valued connection over spectacle.

Her willingness to tackle difficult issues, from mental health to relationships to social justice, has made her a trusted voice for many. She is not just a presenter; she is a confidante, an advocate, and a beacon of resilience in an industry that often lacks compassion. Her career is a testament to the idea that success is not measured by accolades or ratings alone, but by the impact you have on the lives of others.

Looking ahead, Vanessa Feltz will undoubtedly continue to be a fixture in British media for years to come. Her voice is one that the public has come to rely on—whether for a morning pick-me-up, a thoughtful reflection on the issues of the day, or a candid conversation about the realities of life in the spotlight. As she continues to evolve both personally and professionally, Vanessa remains an enduring symbol of strength, resilience, and authenticity in the often fickle world of show business.

In a media landscape that is constantly changing, Vanessa Feltz's ability to adapt while remaining true to herself has ensured her longevity. She has weathered storms that would have sunk others, emerging each time stronger and more determined. Her career is a reminder that success is not linear, but the result of persistence, passion, and a willingness to grow.

Vanessa Feltz is more than just a media personality—she is a woman who has lived her life in the public eye with grace, humor, and an unshakeable belief in the power of communication. She has entertained, informed, and inspired millions of people over the course of her career, leaving an indelible mark on British culture. As she continues her journey, one thing is certain: Vanessa Feltz will remain a beloved figure, not just for her talents as a broadcaster, but for her humanity.

This is Vanessa's legacy—a story of reinvention, resilience, and an unwavering commitment to the truth, no matter how difficult it may be to tell.

Printed in Great Britain
by Amazon